TWO WORLDS, AND OTHER POEMS

By R. W. GILDER

I. THE NEW DAY
II. THE CELESTIAL PASSION
III. LYRICS
IV. TWO WORLDS, AND OTHER POEMS

TWO WORLDS ❀ AND OTHER POEMS ❀ BY RICHARD WATSON GILDER

PUBLISHED BY THE
CENTURY CO. N. Y.
1891

The De Vinne Press.

CONTENTS

I

II

III

IV

V

Decorations by H. de K.

I

TWO WORLDS

I

THE VENUS OF MILO

GRACE, majesty, and the calm bliss of life;
No conscious war 'twixt human will and duty;
Here breathes, forever free from pain and strife,
The old, untroubled pagan world of beauty.

II

MICHAEL ANGELO'S SLAVE

OF life, of death the mystery and woe,
Witness in this mute, carven stone the whole.
That suffering smile were never fashioned so
Before the world had wakened to a soul.

II

THE STAR IN THE CITY

AS down the city street
  I pass at the twilight hour,
'Mid the noise of wheels and hoofs
That grind on the stones, and beat,—
Upward, by spire and tower,
Over the chimneys and roofs
Climbs my glance to the skies,
And I see, with a glad surprise,
A mist with a core of light.
  Slowly, as grows the night,—
As the sky turns blue from gray,—
Slowly it beams more bright,
And keeps with me on my way.
  Soul of the twilight star
That leads me from afar,

Spirit that keener glows
As the daylight darker grows,—
That leaps the chasm of blue
Where the cross-street thunders through,
And follows o'er roof and spire,
In the night-time soaring higher;
I know thee, and only I,—
Thou comrade of the sky,—
Star of the poet's heart,
The light and soul of his art.

MOONLIGHT

'T IS twelve o' the clock.
  The town is still;
As gray as a rock
  From gable to sill
Each cottage is standing.
  The narrow street
  (Where the tree-tops meet),
From the woods to the landing,
Is black with shadows;
  The roofs are white,
And white are the meadows;
  The harbor is bright:
  Can this be night?

II

'Tis twelve o' the clock.
  The town is still;
As still as a stock
  From harbor to hill.
The moon's broad marge
  Has no stars near,
  Far off how clear
They shine, how large!
Something is strange
  In the air, in the light;
Come forth! Let us range
  In the black, in the white,
  Through the day-like night.

III

In the elm trees all
  No flutter, no twitter;
From the granite wall
  The small stars glitter.

A filmy thread
  My forehead brushes;
  A meteor rushes
From green to red.
Naught is but the bliss
  Of this dark, of this white,
Of these stars,—of this kiss,
  O my Love and my Light
  In the day and the night.

"I CARE NOT IF THE SKIES ARE WHITE"

I CARE not if the skies are white,
    Nor if the fields are gold;
I care not whether 't is black or bright,
    Or winds blow soft or cold;
        But O the dark, dark woods,
        For thee, and me, and love.

Let all but us at last depart,
    The great world say farewell!
This is the kingdom of the heart,
    Where only three may dwell;
        And O the dark, dark woods,
        For thee, and me, and love.

CONTRASTS

I

THUNDER in the north sky,
  Sunshine in the south;
Frowning eyes and forehead
  And a smiling mouth.

II

Maiden in the morning,—
  Love her! Yes—but fear her!
In the moony shadows—
  Nearer, nearer, nearer!

SERENADE

(FOR MUSIC)

I

DEEP in the ocean of night
  A pearl through the darkness shines;
Asleep in the garden of night
  A lily's head reclines;
Afar in the forest of night
  Dreams the nightingale;
Clouds in the sky of night
  Make one bright star grow pale.

II

O thou, sweet soul of my love,
  Art my pearl, my lily-flower;
Thou, hiding heart of my love,

Art my bird, in thy maiden bower;
Heart of my only love
That shin'st in the heavens afar—
Thou, in the night of love,
Art my one, dear, trembling star.

III

Let me draw thee to the light
Pearl of the shadowy sea!
Awake, thou lily of light,
Turn thy face divine on me!
Arouse thee, bird of the night,
Let thy voice to my voice reply!
Star of thy lover's night,
Shine forth or I die—I die!

LARGESS

I

SWEET mouth, dark eyes, deep heart,—
  All of beauty, all of glamour heaven could fashion
With its divinest art;
  A woman's life and love, a woman's passion:

II

But these, at last, to win,
  Land, or sea, or hell, or heaven might well be ravished
At price of any sin,—
  Yet freely all she on her lover lavished.

INDOORS, AT NIGHT

THE window's white, the candle's red,
Show evening falleth overhead;
The candle's red, the window's black,
And earth is close in midnight's sack;
The candle fades,
The midnight shades
Turn suddenly a starry blue —
And now to dreams, my soul, of you!

THE ABSENT LOVER

THE purple of the summer fields, the dark
Of forests, and the upward mountain sweep—
Broken by crags, and scar of avalanche;
The trembling of the tops of million trees;
A world of sunlight thrilled with winds of dawn;
All these I feel, I breathe, all these I am
When with closed eyes I bring thy presence near,
And touch thy spirit with my spirit's love.

"TO-NIGHT THE MUSIC DOTH A BURDEN BEAR"

TO-NIGHT the music doth a burden bear,—
One word that moans and murmurs; doth exhale
Tremulously as perfume on the air
From out a rose blood-red, or lily pale;
The burden is thy name, dear soul of me,
Which the rapt melodist unknowing all
Still doth repeat through fugue and reverie;
Thy name, to him unknown, to me doth call—
And weeps my heart at every music-fall.

SANCTUM SANCTORUM

I

I THOUGHT I knew the mountain's every mood,
Gray, black with storms, or lit by lightening dawn;
But once in evening twilight came a spell
Upon its brow, that held me with new power;
A look of unknown beauty, a deep mood
Touched with a sorrow as of human kind.

II

I thought I knew full well my comrade's face,
But a new face it was to me this day.
She sat among the worshipers and heard
The preacher's voice, yet listened not, but leaned
Her head unto a tone whose accents fell
On her sweet spirit only. Deep the awe
Struck then upon me, for my friend no more

Seemed to be near, as with forgetting gaze,
And piteous features steeped in tenderness,
She thought on things unspeakable,—unknown
To all the world beside.

III

When forth doth pass
In holy pilgrimage and awful quest,
The soul of thy soul's comrade, thou must stand
In silence by, and let it move alone
And unattended far to the inner shrine:
Thou canst but wait, and bow thine head, and pray;
And well for thee if thou may'st prove so pure,—
Ended that hour,—thy comrade thou regain'st,
Thine as before, or even more deeply thine.

"AH, TIME, GO NOT SO SOON"

Ah, Time, go not so soon,
I would not thus be used, I would forego that boon;
Turn back, swift Time, and let
Me many a year forget;
Let her be strange once more,—an unfamiliar tune,
An unimagined flower,
Not known till that mute, wondrous hour
When first we met!

THE GIFT

I

Life came to me and spoke:
" A palace for thee I have built
Wherein to take thy pleasure;
I have filled it with priceless treasure;
Seven days shalt thou dwell therein,
Thy joy shall be keener than sin,
Without the stain of guilt—
Enter the door of oak! "

II

I entered the oaken door;
Within, no ray of light,
I saw no golden store,
My heart stood still with fright;

To curse Life was I fain;
Then one unseen before
Laid in my own her hand,
And said: "Come thou and know
This is the House of Woe,—
I am Life's sister, Pain."

III

Through many a breathless way
In dark, on dizzying height,
She led me through the day
And into the dreadful night;
My soul was sore distressed
And wildly I longed for rest;—
Till a chamber met my sight,
Far off, and hid, and still,
With diamonds all bedight
And every precious thing;
Not even a god might will
More beauty there to bring.

IV

Then spoke Life's sister, Pain,
"Here thou as a king shalt reign,
Here shalt thou take thy pleasure,
This is the priceless treasure,
The chamber of thy delight
Through endless day and night;
Rejoice, this is the end:
Thou hast found the heart of a friend."

"THE YEARS ARE ANGELS"

The years are angels that bring down from Heaven
Gifts of the gods. What has the angel given
Who last night vanished up the heavenly wall?
He gave a friend — the gods' best gift of all.

"IN HER YOUNG EYES"

In her young eyes the children looked and found
Their happy comrade. Summer souls false-bound
In age's frosty winter,— without ruth,—
Lived once again in her their long-lost youth.

"YESTERDAY, WHEN WE WERE FRIENDS"

I

Yesterday, when we were friends,
We were scarcely friends at all;
Now we have been friends so long,
And our love has grown so strong.

II

When to-morrow's eve shall fall
We shall say, as night descends,
Again shall say: Ah, yesterday
Scarcely were we friends at all—
Now we have been friends so long
Our love has grown so deep, so strong.

A NIGHT SONG

(FOR THE GUITAR)

THE leaves are dark and large, Love,
'Tis blue at every marge, Love;

The stars hang in the tree, Love,
I 'll pluck them all for thee, Love;

The crescent moon is curled, Love,
Down at the edge of the world, Love;

I 'll run and bring it now, Love,
To crown thy gentle brow, Love;

For in my song
The summer long

The stars, and moon, and night, Love,
Are but for thy delight, Love!

LEO

I

OVER the roofs of the houses I hear the barking of Leo —
Leo the shaggy, the lustrous, the giant, the gentle New-
foundland.
Dark are his eyes as the night, and black is his hair as the
midnight;
Large and slow is his tread till he sees his master re-
turning,
Then how he leaps in the air, with motion ponderous,
frightening!
Now as I pass to my work I hear o'er the roar of the
city —
Far over the roofs of the houses, I hear the barking of
Leo;
For me he is moaning and crying, for me in measure
sonorous
He raises his marvelous voice, for me he is wailing and
calling.

II

None can assuage his grief though but for a day is the
parting,
Though morn after morn 't is the same, though home
every night comes his master,
Still will he grieve when we sever, and wild will be his
rejoicing
When at night his master returns and lays but a hand on
his forehead.
No lack will there be in the world of faith, of love, and
devotion,
No lack for me and for mine, while Leo alone is living—
While over the roofs of the houses I hear the barking of
Leo.

III

BROTHERS

PASSION is a wayward child,
Art his brother firm and mild.
Lonely each
Doth fail to reach
Height of music, song or speech.
If hand in hand they sally forth,
East or west, or south or north,
Naught can stay them
Nor delay them.
Slaves not they of space or time
In their journeyings sublime.

LOVE, ART, AND TIME

ON A PICTURE ENTITLED "THE PORTRAIT," BY WILL H. LOW

SWEET Grecian girl who on the sunbright wall
Tracest the outline of thy lover's shade,
While, on the dial near, Time's hand is laid
With silent motion — fearest thou, then, all?
How that one day the light shall cease to fall
On him who is thy light; how lost, dismayed,—
By Time, and Time's pale comrade, Death betrayed,—
Thou shalt breathe on beneath the all-shadowing pall!

Love, Art, and Time — these are the triple powers
That rule the world, and shall for many a morrow:
Love that beseecheth Art to conquer Time!
Bright is the picture, but, O fading flowers!
O youth that passes, love that bringeth sorrow —
Bright is the picture; sad the poet's rhyme.

THE DANCERS

ON A PICTURE ENTITLED "SUMMER," BY T. W. DEWING

Behold these maidens in a row
Against the birches' freshening green;
Their lines like music sway and flow;
They move before the emerald screen
Like broidered figures dimly seen
On woven cloths, in moony glow—
Gracious, and graceful, and serene.
They hear the harp; its lovely tones
Each maiden in each motion owns,
As if she were a living note
Which from that curvéd harp doth float.

THE TWENTY-THIRD OF APRIL

A LITTLE English earth and breathéd air
Made Shakespeare the divine; so is his verse
The broidered soil of every blossom fair;
So doth his song all sweet bird-songs rehearse.
But tell me, then, what wondrous stuff did fashion
That part of him which took those wilding flights
Among imagined worlds; whence the white passion
That burned three centuries through the days and nights!
Not heaven's four winds could make, nor the round earth,
The soul wherefrom the soul of Hamlet flamed:
Nor anything of merely mortal birth
Could lighten as when Shakespeare's name is named.
How was his body bred we know full well,
But that high soul's engendering who may tell!

EMMA LAZARUS

When on thy bed of pain thou layest low
Daily we saw thy body fade away,
Nor could the love wherewith we loved thee stay
For one dear hour the flesh borne down by woe;
But as the mortal sank, with what white glow
Flamed thy eternal spirit, night and day —
Untouched, unwasted, though the crumbling clay
Lay wrecked and ruined! Ah, is it not so,
Dear poet-comrade, who from sight hast gone —
Is it not so that spirit hath a life
Death may not conquer? But, O dauntless one!
Still must we sorrow. Heavy is the strife
And thou not with us — thou of the old race
That with Jehovah parleyed, face to face.

THE TWELFTH OF DECEMBER

On this day Browning died?
Say, rather: On the tide
That throbs against those glorious palace walls;
That rises—pauses—falls
With melody, and myriad-tinted gleams;
On that enchanted tide,
Half real, and half poured from lovely dreams,
A Soul of Beauty,—a white, rhythmic flame,—
Passed singing forth into the Eternal Beauty whence
it came.

IV

SHERIDAN

I

QUIETLY, like a child
That sinks in slumber mild,
No pain or troubled thought his well-earned peace to mar,
Sank into endless rest our thunder-bolt of war.

II

Though his the power to smite
Quick as the lightning's light,—
His single arm an army, and his name a host,—
Not his the love of blood, the warrior's cruel boast.

III

But in the battle's flame
How glorious he came!—
Even like a white-combed wave that breaks and tears the shore,
While wreck lies strewn behind, and terror flies before.

IV

'T was he,—his voice, his might,—
Could stay the panic-flight,
Alone shame back the headlong, many-leagued retreat,
And turn to evening triumph morning's foul defeat.

V

He was our modern Mars;
Yet firm his faith that wars
Erelong would cease to vex the sad, ensanguined earth,
And peace forever reign, as at Christ's holy birth.

VI

Blest land, in whose dark hour
Arise to loftiest power
No dazzlers of the sword to play the tyrant's part,
But patriot-soldiers, true and pure and high of heart!

VII

Of such our chief of all;
And he who broke the wall
Of civil strife in twain, no more to build or mend;
And he who hath this day made Death his faithful friend.

VIII

And now above his tomb
From out the eternal gloom
"Welcome!" his chieftain's voice sounds o'er the cannon's knell;
And of the three one only stays to say "Farewell!"

SHERMAN

I

Glory and honor and fame and everlasting laudation
For our captains who loved not war, but fought for the
    life of the nation;
Who knew that, in all the land, one slave meant strife,
    not peace;
Who fought for freedom, not glory; made war that
    war might cease.

II

Glory and honor and fame;— the beating of muffled
    drums;
The wailing funeral dirge, as the flag-wrapped coffin
    comes.
Fame and honor and glory, and joy for a noble soul;
For a full and splendid life, and laureled rest at the
    goal.

III

Glory and honor and fame;— the pomp that a soldier
prizes;
The league-long waving line as the marching falls and
rises;
Rumbling of caissons and guns, the clatter of horses'
feet,
And a million awe-struck faces far down the waiting
street.

IV

But better than martial woe, and the pageant of civic
sorrow;
Better than praise of to-day, or the statue we build to-
morrow;
Better than honor and glory, and history's iron pen,
Is the thought of duty done and the love of his fellow-
men.

PRO PATRIA

IN MEMORY OF A FAITHFUL CHAPLAIN*

I

EREWHILE I sang the praise of them whose lustrous names
Flashed in war's dreadful flames;
Who rose in glory, and in splendor, and in might
To fame's sequestered height.

II

Honor to all, for each his honors meekly carried,
Nor e'er the conquered harried;
All honor, for they sought alone to serve the state —
Not merely to be great.

* The chaplain referred to lost his life through taking upon himself the visitation of the army smallpox hospital, near the camp of his regiment, the 40th N. Y. Vols., at Brandy Station, Virginia, April, 1864.

III

Yes, while the glorious past our grateful memory
craves,
And while yon bright flag waves,
Lincoln, Grant, Sherman, Sheridan, the peerless four,
Shall live forever more;

IV

Shall shine the eternal stars of stern and loyal love,
All other stars above;
The imperial nation they made one, at last, and free,
Their monument shall be.

V

Ah yes! but ne'er may we forget the praise to sound
Of the brave souls that found
Death in the myriad ranks, 'mid blood, and groans,
and stenches —
Tombs in the abhorred trenches.

VI

Comrades! To-day a tear-wet garland I would bring—
But one song let me sing,
For one sole hero of my heart and desolate home;
Come with me, Comrades, come!

VII

Bring your glad flowers, your flags, for this one humble grave;
For, Soldiers, he was brave!
Though fell not he before the cannon's thunderous breath,
Yet noble was his death.

VIII

True soldier of his country and the sacred cross,—
He counted gain, not loss,
Perils and nameless horrors of the embattled field,
While he had help to yield.

IX

But not where 'mid wild cheers the awful battle broke,—
A hell of fire and smoke,—
He to heroic death went forth with soul elate—
Harder his lonely fate.

X

Searching where most was needed, worst of all endured,
Sufferers he found immured,—
Tented apart because of fatal, foul disease,—
Balm brought he unto these:

XI

Celestial balm, the spirit's holy ministry,
He brought, and only he;
Where men who blanched not at the battle's shell and shot
Trembled, and entered not.

XII

Yet life to him was oh, most dear,—home, children, wife,—
But, dearer still than life,
Duty—that passion of the soul which from the sod
Alone lifts man to God.

XIII

The pest-house entering fearless—stricken he fearless fell,
Knowing that all was well:
The high, mysterious Power whereof mankind has dreamed
To him not distant seemed.

XIV

So nobly died this unknown hero of the war;
And heroes, near and far,
Sleep now in graves like his unfamed in song or story—
But theirs is more than glory!

FAILURE AND SUCCESS

HE fails who climbs to power and place
Up the pathway of disgrace.
He fails not who makes truth his cause,
Nor bends to win the crowd's applause.
He fails not, he who stakes his all
Upon the right, and dares to fall;—
What though the living bless or blame,
For him the long success of fame.

J. R. L.

ON HIS BIRTHDAY

NAVIES nor armies can exalt the state,—
  Millions of men, nor coinèd wealth untold:
  Down to the pit may sink a land of gold;
But one great name can make a country great.

NAPOLEON

A soul inhuman? No — but human all,
  If human is each passion man has known:
  Scorn, hate, and love ; the lust of empire, grown
  To such a height as did the world appal;—
If the same human soul may soar and crawl
  As soared his and as crawled; if to be shown
  The utmost heaven and hell; if to atone
  For fame consummate by colossal fall;—
If human 't is to see friend, partisan
  Turn, dastardly, the imperial hand to tear
  That fed them; if through gnawing years to plan
Vengeance, and space to breathe the unfettered air,—
  No alien from his kind but very man
  Slow perished on that island of despair.

THE WHITE TSAR'S PEOPLE

PART I

THE White Tsar's people cry:
"Thou God of the heat and the cold,
Of storm and of lightning,
Of darkness, and dawn's red brightening;
Hold, Lord God, hold,
Hold Thy hand lest we curse Thee and die."

The White Tsar's people pray:
"Thou God of the South and the North,
We are crushed, we are bleeding;
'T is Christ, 't is Thy Son interceding;
Forth, Lord, come forth!
Bid the slayer no longer slay."

The White Tsar's people call
Aloud to the skies of lead:
"We are slaves, not freemen;
Ourselves, our children, our women,—
Dead, we are dead,
Though we breathe, we are dead men all.

"Blame not if we misprize thee
Who can, but will not draw near.
'Tis Thou who hast made us—
Not Thou, dread God, to upbraid us.
Hear, Lord God, hear!
Lest we whom Thou madest despise Thee."

PART II

Then answered the most high God,
Lord of the heat and the cold,
Of storm and of lightning,
Of darkness, and dawn's red brightening:
"Bold, yea, too bold,
Whom I wrought from the air and the clod!

" Hast thou forgotten from me
Are those ears so quick to hear
The passion and anguish
Of your sisters, your children who languish
Near? Ah, not near —
Far off by the uttermost sea!

" Who gave ye your hearts to bleed
And brains to weave and to plan?
Why call ye on heaven —
'T is the earth that to you is given!
Plead, ye may plead,
But for man I work through man.

" Who gave ye a voice to utter
Your tale to the wind and the sea?
One word well spoken
And the iron gates are broken.
From me, yea, from me
The word that ye will not mutter.

"I love not murder but ruth.
Begone from my sight ye who take
The knife of the coward —
Even ye who by heaven were dowered!
Wake ye, O wake,
And strike with the sword of Truth!

"Fear ye lest I misprize ye —
I who fashioned not brutes, but men.
After the lightning
And darkness — the dawn's red brightening!
Men! Be ye men!
Lest I who made ye despise ye!"

V

5

HIDE NOT THY HEART

I

THIS is my creed,
This be my deed:
"Hide not thy heart!"
Soon we depart;
Mortals are all,
A breath, then the pall;
A flash on the dark —
All 's done — stiff and stark.
No time for a lie;
The truth, and then die.
Hide not thy heart!

II

Forth with thy thought!
Soon 't will be naught,
And thou in thy tomb.
Now is air, now is room.
Down with false shame;
Reck not of fame;
Dread not man's spite;
Quench not thy light.
This be thy creed,
This be thy deed:
"Hide not thy heart!"

III

If God is, he made
Sunshine and shade,
Heaven and hell;
This we know well.
Dost thou believe?
Do not deceive;

Scorn not thy faith:
If 't is a wraith,
Soon it will fly.
Thou, who must die,
Hide not thy heart!

IV

This is my creed,
This be my deed!
Faith, or a doubt —
I shall speak out
And hide not my heart.

"THE POET FROM HIS OWN SORROW"

THE poet from his own sorrow
  Poured forth a love-sad song.
A stranger, on the morrow,
  Drew near, with a look of wrong,
And said — "Beneath its pall
  I have hidden my heart in vain —
To the world thou hast sung it all!
  Who told thee my secret pain?"

"WHITE, PILLARED NECK"

WHITE, pillared neck; a brow to make men quake;
  A woman's perfect form;—
Like some cool marble, should that wake,
  Breathe, and be warm.

A shape, a mind, a heart—
  Of womanhood the whole:
Her breath, her smile, her touch, her art,
  All—save her soul.

"GREAT NATURE IS AN ARMY GAY"

Great nature is an army gay,
Resistless marching on its way;
I hear the bugles clear and sweet,
I hear the tread of million feet.
  Across the plain I see it pour;
It tramples down the waving grass;
Within the echoing mountain pass
I hear a thousand cannon roar.
  It swarms within my garden gate;
My deepest well it drinketh dry.
It doth not rest; it doth not wait;
By night and day it sweepeth by;
Ceaseless it marches by my door;
It heeds me not, though I implore.
I know not whence it comes, nor where
It goes. For me it doth not care —

Whether I starve, or eat, or sleep,
Or live, or die, or sing, or weep.
And now the banners all are bright,
Now torn and blackened by the fight.
Sometimes its laughter shakes the sky,
Sometimes the groans of those who die.
Still through the night and through the livelong day
The infinite army marches on its remorseless way.

"LIFE IS THE COST"

I

LIFE is the cost.
Behold yon tower,
That heavenward lifts
To the cloudy drifts —
Like a flame, like a flower!
What lightness, what grace,
What a dream of power!
One last endeavor
One stone to place —
And it stands forever.

II

A slip, a fall —
A cry, a call;
Turn away — all 's done.
Stands the tower in the sun

Forever and a day.
On the pavement below
The crimson stain
Will be worn away
In the ebb and flow;—
The tower will remain.
Life is the cost.

THE PRISONER'S THOUGHT

I

Is 'T I for whom the law's brute penalty
Was made,—to whom the law once seemed a power
Far off and not to be concerned withal?
Am I indeed this rank and noisome thing
Fit for such handling—to be pushed aside
Into a human foul receptacle,
A fetid compost of dull festering crime
Even not fit for nutriment of the earth,
But only here to rot in memories
Of my own shame, and shame of other men?
  Here let me rot then—there 's a taste one has
For just the best of all things, even of sin.
He 's a poor devil who in deepest hell
Knows no keen relish for the worst that is,—
The very acme of intensest pain,—
Nor smacks charred lips at thoughts of some dear
    crime,

The sweetest, deadliest, damnablest of all.
Sometimes I hug that hellish happiness;
And then a loathing falls upon my soul
For what I was, and am, and still must be.

II

And this same I,—there comes to me a time,
And often comes, when all this slips away;
Stays not one stain, nor scar, nor fatal hurt.
Perhaps it is a sort of waking dream;
But if I dream, I 'm breathing audibly,
I feel my pulse beat, hear the talk and tread
Down these long corridors; see the barred blue
Of the cell's window, hear a singing bird—
Yes, O my God, I hear a singing bird,
Such as I heard in childhood. Now, you think,
I dream I am a child once more. Not so;
I am just what I am; a man in prison—
(Damn them! I 'm innocent of what they swore
And proved—with cant, and well-paid perjury;
Though other crimes, they know not of, I did)—
But suddenly my soul is pure as yours;

My thoughts as clean; my spirit is as free
As any man's, or any purest woman's.
I think as justly, as for instance, sir,
You think; as circumspectly, wisely, freely,
As does my genial keeper, or the smith
Who enters once a day to try the bars
That shut my body out from freedom! Not
My soul. Why, this my soul has thoughts that strike
Into the very heights and depths of Heaven.
You 'll think it passing strange, good friend, no doubt.
'T is strange; but here 's a further mystery:
Think you that in some other living state
After what we call death, — or in this life,—
The thinking part of us we name the soul
Can ever get away from its old self;
Can wash the earth all off from it, that so
It really will be, what I sometimes seem —
As sinless as a little child at birth,
With all a woman's love for all things pure,
And all a grown man's strength to do the right?

THE CONDEMNED

THOU art not fit to die? — Why not?
The fairest body ripes to rot;
Thy soul? Oh, why not let it go
Free from the flesh that drags it low!
To die! Poor wretch, do not deceive
Thyself — who art not fit to live.

"SOW THOU SORROW"

Sow thou sorrow and thou shalt reap it;
Sow thou joy and thou shalt keep it.

TEMPTATION

Not alone in pain and gloom,
Does the abhorréd tempter come;
Not in light alone and pleasure
Proffers he the poisoned measure.
  When the soul doth rise
Nearest to its native skies,
There the exalted spirit finds
Borne upon the heavenly winds
Satan, in an angel's guise,
With voice divine and innocent eyes.

A MIDSUMMER MEDITATION

I

FACE once the thought: This piled up sky of cloud,
Blue vastness, and white vastness steeped in light, —
Struck through with light, that centers in the sun, —
This blue of waves below that meets blue sky:
But a white, trembling shore between, that sweeps
The circle of the bay; this green of woods,
And keener green of new-mown, grassy fields;
This ceaseless, leaf-like rustle of the waves;
These shining, billowy tree-tops; songs of birds;
Strong scent of seaweed, mixed with smell of pines;
Face once this thought: Thy spirit that looks forth,
That breathes the light, and life, and joy of all,
Shall cease, but not the things that pleasure thee;
They shall endure for eyes like thine, but not
For thine own eyes; for human hearts like thine,
But not for thine own heart, all dust and dead.

II

Face it, O Spirit, then look up once more,
Brave conqueror of dull mortality!
Look up and be a part of all thou see'st;—
Ocean and earth and miracle of sky,
All that thou see'st, is thee, and without thee
Were naught. Thou, too, a god, dost recreate
The whole; breathing thy soul on all, till all
Is one wide world made perfect at thy touch.
And know that thou, who darest a world create,
Art one with the Almighty, son to sire—
Of his eternity a quenchless spark.

"AS DOTH THE BIRD"

As doth the bird, on outstretched pinions, dare
The dread abysm's viewless air —
Take thou, my soul, thy fearless flight
Into the void and dark of death's eternal night.

In the Catskills.

VISIONS

I

Cast into the pit
Of lonely sorrow,
The suffering soul,
Looking aloft,
Sees with amaze
In the day-time sky
The shine of stars.

II

Came to me once
In the seething town
A form of beauty,
Innocent brow,
And soul of youth;

Deep, sweet eyes,
An angel's gaze,
And rose-leaf lips
That murmured low:
"I am thy sin."

III

With full-toned beat
Of the happy heart,
In a day of peace,
In an hour of joy,
Once in my life
And only once,
Of a sudden, I saw,
The end of all!
——Death!

WITH A CROSS OF IMMORTELLES

WHEN Christ cried, "It is done!"
  The face of a small red flower,
Looking up to the suffering One,
      Turned pale with love and pain,
      And never shone red again.
  In memory of that hour
Which holds the secret of bliss,
  And the darker secret of sorrow —
  That shall come to each, to-morrow —
Sweet friend, I send you this.

THE PASSING OF CHRIST

I

O Man of light and lore!
Do you mean that in our day
The Christ has passed away;
That nothing now is divine
In the fierce rays that shine
Through every cranny and thought;
That Christ as he once was taught
Shall be the Christ no more?
That the Hope and Saviour of men
Shall be seen no more again;
That, miracles being done,
Gone is the Holy One?
And thus, you hold, the Christ
For the past alone sufficed;

From the throne of the hearts of the world
The Son of God shall be hurled,
And henceforth must be sought
New prophets and kings of thought;
That the tenderest, truest word
The heart of sorrow had heard
Shall sound no more on earth;
That he who has made of birth
A dread and holy rite;
Who has brought to the eyes of death
A vision of heavenly light,
Shall fade with our failing faith;—
He who saw in children's eyes
Eternal paradise;
Who looked through shame and sin
At the sanctity within;
Whose memory, since he died,
The earth has sanctified—
Has been the stay and the hold
Of millions of lives untold,
And the world on its upward path
Has led from crime and wrath;—

You say that this Christ has passed
And we can not hold him fast.

II

Ah no! If the Christ you mean
Shall pass from this time, this scene,
These hearts, these lives of ours,
'T is but as the summer flowers
Pass, but return again,
To gladden the world of men.
For he,—the only, the true,—
In each age, in each waiting heart,
Leaps into life anew;
Though he pass, he shall not depart.

Behold him now where he comes!
Not the Christ of our subtile creeds,
But the light of our hearts, of our homes,
Of our hopes, our prayers, our needs;
The brother of want and blame,
The lover of women and men,

With a love that puts to shame
All passions of mortal ken:
Yet of all of woman born
His is the scorn of scorn;
Before whose face doth fly
Lies, and the love of a lie;
Who from the temple of God,
And the sacred place of laws,
Drives forth, with uplifted rod,
The herds of ravening maws.

'T is he, as none other can,
Makes free the spirit of man,
And speaks, in darkest night,
One word of awful light
That strikes through the dreadful pain
Of life, a reason sane—
That word divine which brought
The universe from naught.

Ah no, thou life of the heart,
Never shalt thou depart!

Not till the leaven of God
Shall lighten each human clod;
Not till the world shall climb
To thy height serene, sublime,
Shall the Christ who enters our door
Pass to return no more.

CREDO

How easily my neighbor chants his creed,
Kneeling beside me in the House of God.
His "I believe" he chants, and "I believe,"
With cheerful iteration and consent—
Watching meantime the white, slow sunbeam move
Across the aisle, or listening to the bird
Whose free, wild song sounds through the open door.

Thou God supreme,—I too, I too, believe!
But oh! forgive if this one human word,
Binding the deep and breathless thought of thee
And my own conscience with an iron band,
Stick in my throat. I cannot say it, thus—
This "I believe" that doth thyself obscure;
This rod to smite; this barrier; this blot
On thy most unimaginable face
And soul of majesty.

'T is not man's faith
In thee that he proclaims in formal phrase,
But faith in man; faith not in thine own Christ,
But in another man's dim thought of him.

Christ of Judea, look thou in my heart.
Do I not love thee, look to thee, in thee
Alone have faith of all the sons of men! —
Faith deepening with the weight and woe of years:

Pure soul and tenderest of all that came
Into this world of sorrow, hear my prayer:

Lead me, yea lead me deeper into life —
This suffering, human life wherein thou liv'st
And breathest still, and hold'st thy way divine.
'T is here, O pitying Christ, where thee I seek,
Here where the strife is fiercest; where the sun
Beats down upon the highway thronged with men,
And in the raging mart. Oh! deeper lead
My soul into the living world of souls
Where thou dost move.

But lead me, Man Divine,
Where'er thou will'st, only that I may find
At the long journey's end thy image there,
And grow more like to it. For art not thou
The human shadow of the infinite Love
That made and fills the endless universe!
The very Word of him, the unseen, unknown
Eternal Good that rules the summer flower
And all the worlds that people starry space!

NON SINE DOLORE

I

WHAT, then, is Life,— what Death?
Thus the Answerer saith;
O faithless mortal, bend thy head and listen:

Down o'er the vibrant strings,
That thrill, and moan, and mourn, and glisten,
The Master draws his bow.
A voiceless pause; then upward, see, it springs,
Free as a bird with unimprisoned wings!
In twain the chord was cloven,
While, shaken with woe,
With breaks of instant joy all interwoven,
Piercing the heart with lyric knife,
On, on the ceaseless music sings,
Restless, intense, serene:
Life is the downward stroke; the upward, Life;
Death but the pause between.

II

Then spake the Questioner: If 't were only this,
Ah, who could face the abyss
That plunges down athwart each human breath?
If the new birth of Death
Meant only more of Life as mortals know it,
What priestly balm, what song of highest poet,
Could heal one sentient soul's immitigable pain?
All, all were vain!
If, having soared pure spirit at the last,
Free from the impertinence and warp of flesh,
We find half joy, half pain, on every blast,
Are caught again in closer-woven mesh,—
Ah! who would care to die
From out these fields and hills, and this familiar sky;
These firm, sure hands that compass us, this dear
humanity?

III

Again the Answerer saith:
O ye of little faith,

Shall, then, the spirit prove craven,
And Death's divine deliverance but give
A summer rest and haven?
By all most noble in us, by the light that streams
Into our waking dreams,
Ah, we who know what Life is, let us live!
Clearer and freeer, who shall doubt?
Something of dust and darkness cast forever out;
But Life, still Life, that leads to higher Life,—
Even though the highest be not free from the immortal strife.

The highest! Soul of man, oh, be thou bold,
And to the brink of thought draw near, behold!
Where, on the earth's green sod,
Where, where in all the universe of God,
Hath strife forever ceased?
When hath not some great orb flashed into space
The terror of its doom? When hath no human face
Turned earthward in despair,
For that some horrid sin had stamped its image there?

If at our passing Life be Life increased,
And we ourselves flame pure unfettered soul,
Like the eternal power that made the whole
And lives in all he made
From shore of matter to the unknown spirit shore;
If, sire to son, and tree to limb,
Cycle by countless cycle more and more
We grow to be like him;
If he lives on, serene and unafraid
Through all his light, his love, his living thought,
One with the sufferer, be it soul or star;
If he escape not pain,—what beings that are
Can e'er escape while Life leads on and up the
unseen way and far?
If he escape not, by whom all was wrought,
Then shall not we,—
Whate'er of godlike solace still may be,—
For in all worlds there is no Life without a pang,
and can be naught.

No Life without a pang! It were not Life,
If ended were the strife—

Man were not man, nor God were truly God!
  See from the sod
The lark thrill skyward in an arrow of song:
Even so from pain and wrong
Upsprings the exultant spirit, wild and free.
He knows not all the joy of liberty
Who never yet was crushed 'neath heavy woe.
He doth not know,
Nor can, the bliss of being brave
Who never hath faced death, nor with unquailing eye
    hath measured his own grave.
  Courage, and pity, and divinest scorn—
Self-scorn, self-pity, and high courage of the
    soul;
The passion for the goal;
The strength to never yield though all be lost—
All these are born
Of endless strife. This is the eternal cost
Of every lovely thought that through the portal
Of human minds doth pass with following light.
Blanch not, O trembling mortal!
But with extreme and terrible delight

Know thou the truth,
Nor let thy heart be heavy with false ruth.

No passing burden is our earthly sorrow
That shall depart in some mysterious morrow.
'Tis His one universe where'er we are—
One changeless law from sun to viewless star.
Were sorrow evil here, evil it were forever,
Beyond the scope and help of our most keen endeavor.
God doth not dote,
His everlasting purpose shall not fail:
Here where our ears are weary with the wail
And weeping of the sufferers; there where the Pleiads float,—
Here, there, forever, pain most dread and dire
Doth bring the intensest bliss, the dearest and most sure.
'T is not from Life aside, it doth endure
Deep in the secret heart of all existence.
It is the inward fire,
The heavenly urge, and the divine insistence.

Uplift thine eyes, O Questioner, from the sod!
It were no longer Life,
If ended were the strife;
Man were not man, God were not truly God.

VI

ODE

Read before the Society of the Phi Beta Kappa, Harvard University, June 26, 1890

ODE

I

IN the white midday's full imperious show
  What glorious colors hide from human sight!
  But in the breathing pause 'twixt day and night
Forth stream those prisoned splendors, glow on glow;
    Like billows on they pour
    And beat against the shore
Of cloud-wrought cliffs high as the utmost dome,
To die in purple waves that break on dawns to come.

II

Divine, divine! Oh, breathe no earthlier word!
  Behold the western heavens how swift they flame
  With hues that bring to mortal language shame;
Swelling and pulsing like deep music heard

On sacred summer eves
When the loud organ grieves
Or thrills with lyric life the incensed air,
While 'mid the pillared gloom the people bow in prayer.

III

Now is it some huge bird with monstrous vans
That through the sunset plies its shadowy way,
Catching on outstretched pinions the last play
Of failing tints celestial! See! it spans
Darkly the fading west,
And now its beamy crest
Follows from sight the glittering, golden sun;
And now one mighty wing-beat more, and all is done.

IV

But in those skyey spaces what dread change!
Thus have we seen the mortal turn immortal;
So doth the day's soul die, as through death's portal
The soul of man takes up its heavenward range.

A million orbs endue
The unfathomable blue—
Till, the long miracle of night withdrawn,
The world beholds once more the miracle of dawn.

V

Dawn, eve, and night, the iridescent seas,
Bright moon, enlightening sun, and quivering stars,
The midnight rose whose petals are the bars
Of Boreal lights, the pomp of autumn trees,
The pearl of curvéd shells,
The prismy bow that swells
'Gainst stormy skies,—these witness, these are sign
Of thee, O Spirit of Beauty, eternal and divine!

VI

And fairer still than all,—chief sign of all,—
The naked loveliness in Eden's bower,
Whose flesh blushed back the tint of fruit and flower;
Whose eye reflamed the starlight; who could call

Father and friend the God
That plucked them from the sod;
The Almighty's image, and Creation's height;
Whose deep souls mirrored clear the circling day and night.

VII

Spirit of Beauty! 'neath thy joyful spell
Man hath been ever; therefore doth each breeze
Bring to his trancéd ears glad melodies,—
Voices of birds, the brook's low, silvery bell,—
Wild music manifold,
Which he hath power to hold
His own enchanted harmonies among,
That echo round the world the songs that nature sung.

VIII

And thus all Beautiful in Holiness
Doth Israel stand before the Eternal One;
Striking his harp with rapt, angelic tone,
Till tribes and nations the Unseen God confess:

Knowing that only where
His face makes white the air
Could such seraphic song have mortal birth,—
One saving faith sublime to keep alive on earth.

IX

And therefore with most passionate desire
And longing, man yearned ever to express
Thy majesty, and light, and loveliness,
O Spirit of Beauty, unconsuming fire!
Therefore by ancient Nile
Rose the vast columned aisle,
And on the Athenian Hill the wonder white
Whose shattered ruins are the world's supreme delight.

X

So is it that to thy imperial shore,
Bright Italy! the generations fly,
Even but once to breathe, or ere they die,
Where did a godlike race its soul outpour;

Its birth divine revealing
On glorious wall and ceiling,—
While dome and rhythmic statue, Beauty-wrought,
Declare all human art is but what Heaven hath taught.

XI

Fair Italy! whose dread and peerless height
The song is of the awful Ghibelline:
Poet! who 'mid the threefold dream divine
Didst follow Art and Love to the Central Light!
Tell us, O Dante! tell
What thou dost know so well,
That horror and death are but the shade and foil
Of Beauty, deathless, godlike, and without assoil.

XII

Spirit divine! man falls upon the sod
In awe of thee, in worship and amaze:
Thou older than the mountains, or the blaze
Of sunsets, or the sun; thou old as God:

As God who did create
Long ere man reached his state
All shapes of natural Beauty that men see,
And his wide universe did dedicate to thee.

XIII

—Ye who bear on the torch of living art
In this new world,—saved for some wondrous fate,—
Deem not that ye have come, alas, too late,
But haste right forward with unfailing heart!
Ye shall not rest forlorn,—
Behold, even now, the morn
Rises in splendor from the orient sea,
And the new world shall greet a new divinity.

XIV

Shall greet, ah, who can say! a nobler face
Than from the foam of Cytherean seas:
Loveliness lovelier; mightier harmonies
Of song and color; an intenser grace:

Beauty that shall endure
Like Charis, heavenly-pure;
A Spirit solemn as the starry night,
And full as the triumphant dawn of golden light.

AFTER-SONG

TO ROSAMOND

ROSE of the world,
Bloom of the year,
Birth of the dawn!
By morn's one star
Lighted to life! —
Thou and my songs
Come to the day
Hand clasped in hand:

Flung on this page
May the glow of thy name
Back through each song
Shine with the light
Drawn from the skies,—
Thou birth of the dawn,
Flower of the morn,
Rose of the world!

www.ingramcontent.com/pod-product-compliance
Lightning Source LLC
LaVergne TN
LVHW021428110826
845150LV00007B/2131

9781425507596